# Calm Your Mind

*Break The Cycle Of Anxiety, Stress,
Unhappiness, Exhaustion, And Find Peace In
A Rushed World*

Steven Schuster

steveschusterbooks@gmail.com

professional person should be sought. The author shall not be liable for damages arising herefrom. The fact that an individual, organization of website is referred to in this work as a citation and/or potential source of further information does not mean that the author endorses the information the individual, organization to website may provide or recommendations they/it may make. Further, readers should be aware that Internet websites listed in this work might have changed or disappeared between when this work was written and when it is read.

For general information on the products and services or to obtain technical support, please contact the author.

Table Of Contents

Chapter 1 – What is Mindfulness? ........................9

Chapter 2 - Meditation ........................................21

Chapter 3 – Spartan Discipline And Willpower ...31

Chapter 4 – Befriend Yourself .............................41

Chapter 5 – Do Nothing .......................................51

Chapter 6- Mindfulness and Goal Setting............59

Chapter 7 – Energy Management With
Mindfulness.........................................................69

Chapter 8 – Mindfulness in Your Life Areas ........77

Chapter 9 – If You Can't Cope Alone ...................91

Final Words..........................................................99

Reference ..........................................................101

Endnotes............................................................109

## Chapter 1 – What is Mindfulness?

Have you ever walked into a room and looked around in confusion, wondering why you were in there? Have you ever driven your car and arrived at your destination without remembering how you got there? Or when you checked your watch, did you have to look at it again because you forgot the time? What about if you were asked to share how you spent the first hour of your day? Would you be able to remember it in detail? If not, you are not alone. All of us have been in those very situations more often than we would probably like to admit.

If you, like so many of us, find that you can't remember parts of your day, it doesn't necessarily signal a memory problem. It may just mean that you aren't truly present in your head. Presence is the key to achieving mindfulness.

## What is Mindfulness?

Mindfulness is when our mind is completely focused on the present moment and attentive to what is happening in it. According to mindful.org, "Mindfulness is the basic human ability to be fully present, aware of where we are and what we're doing, and not overly reactive or overwhelmed by what's going on around us." Being mindful is something we are born having the ability to do, but it is not as easy to achieve as one might think.

Focusing our mind for any extended period of time is not something that comes easily and naturally to most of us. Our mind wanders more often than we might even be aware. The majority of the time, our mind drifts into places of negative thoughts which can cause us to feel stress, anxiety, regret, shame, and unhappiness. Did you know that eighty percent of the average person's daily thoughts are negative?[i] We may not understand that we are even having these negative thoughts as they form an unconscious mental chatter that can leave us with a feeling that life is hard, and the struggles that we have to go through aren't worth it.

I experienced this in my own life when my wife was in the hospital with a very serious health condition. I spent countless hours in her hospital room. Every time one of the medical machines that she was hooked up to would make any kind of noise, my mind would instantly shift my focus, and I would find myself feeling a sense of panic and always assuming the worst. It was enough to drive me crazy.

On top of that, every time a doctor or nurse would enter the room, they would always start to share information with me. My mind could absorb the first few things they said, but then I would find myself sort of tuning out, not because I didn't want to hear and learn from everything they had to say, but just the opposite; I wanted so badly to understand everything that I found myself feeling completely overwhelmed by it all. It got so I would have to write down key medical terms they would say and then look them up on my phone after they left the room. Then I could sit in the room when it was quiet and focus on coming up with all of the questions I wanted to ask the nurse or doctor. I would write down my questions and then I would ask them the next time I saw them.

My wife was in the hospital for nearly three months. It really took a toll on me. When I was in the hospital, my mind would wander to all of the things I should be doing and was neglecting at work and at home. When I was teaching, my mind wasn't fully focused there either. I had a hard time really concentrating because I felt guilty that I wasn't at the hospital and that I wasn't being a good husband. Whenever I wasn't at home, I would feel stressed, anxious, and guilty about what I should be doing there to be a good father to my children. No matter where I was, I was never completely present. I was never achieving mindfulness. I was juggling so much and not really doing any area of my life the justice it deserved.

This period of my life triggered the irreversible desire in me to become more mindful, take meditation more seriously, and live each of my days with my loved ones as if it would be the last. Before my wife fell ill, I just half-assed all the things I was preaching about: Meh, meditate because it's good. Meh, be mindful because it's so popular to be these days. Yes, yes, live for the moment, got it. But it was not until I experienced the agony of a three-month-long fear of loss in my wife's hospital room that I actually started to feel the weight of the benefits of these practices. Looking back, those months were very educational and useful to make a permanent change in me. Seems like the other cliché, that loss and pain teach us the greatest lessons, is also true.

The good thing is that mindfulness is something everyone can practice and benefit from. It is a way of life. Mindfulness brings awareness and focus to everything we do, and it helps to cut down on needless stress by eliminating the negative thoughts that creep into our minds when they wander. Any time that we can be more mindful improves our lives for the better.

You don't have to only rely on your personal experiences (or mine) to know that this is true. Science backs it up as well. Mindfulness benefits our health, happiness, work, and relationships. When we achieve mindfulness, we are more innovative, effective, resilient, and are better problem-solvers.

## The Scientific Benefits of Mindfulness

Researchers are becoming more interested in the practice of mindfulness as studies continue to prove its many benefits. Currently research is being conducted to study how the brain responds to mindfulness, how relationships benefit, and how physical and mental health can improve when mindfulness is achieved. The following examples are just a sampling of the studies being conducted to discover how mindfulness enhances our well-being.

**Improves the Brain and Immune System**

A study published in *NeuroReport* in 2005 found that people who meditated long-term showed thicker cortical regions in their brains related to attention and sensory processing than people who did not practice meditation.[ii] The findings went on to suggest that practicing meditation might offset the cortical thinning that naturally occurs as people age. This study is not alone in concluding that the practice of meditation and achieving mindfulness may affect the structure and neural patterns present in the brain. Scientists are now seeing the results extend beyond the meditation sessions and into the daily lives of those who regularly meditate.

A study conducted in 2003 investigated how an eight-week training course on how to practice meditation would impact the brains and immune systems of the participants. It found evidence that an area of the brain connected to positive affect showed increased activation, and that the immune systems were able to produce more antibodies after the participants went through the meditation training.[iii]

Another recent study followed Chinese undergraduates who underwent five days of meditation training for 20 minutes a day. It found that when presented with a stressful laboratory task, the students who were trained in how to meditate showed a faster decrease in levels of the stress hormone cortisol, which indicated that they were better able to regulate stress than a group of students who had received relaxation training. The undergraduates who learned to meditate also reported feeling less anxiety, depression, and anger than their counterparts.[iv]


## Improves Relationships

There is mounting evidence that mindfulness training can improve the quality of a person's relationships. A University of North Carolina at Chapel Hill study found a correlation between couples who practice mindfulness and an enhanced relationship. These couples reported a greater feeling of closeness, increased acceptance of each other, and an overall improvement in general satisfaction with their relationships. A study in 2007 drew a similar conclusion. It showed a connection between the improved quality of communication of couples and the practice of mindfulness.[v]

Practicing mindfulness also benefits familial relationships. Parents of children with developmental disabilities indicated that their mindfulness training resulted in their increased satisfaction with their parenting skills, interacting socially more often with their children, and experiencing less parental stress. The same researchers conducted a study in 2006 investigating parents of children with autism and the same results demonstrating an increased satisfaction with their parenting skills and relationships applied. Both studies showed that the children benefitted from their parents practicing mindfulness, as the children themselves showed a decrease in aggressive and non-compliant behavior.[vi]

**Improves Fields of Education**

Studies are now being conducted to see if having children practice mindfulness in an educational setting may prove beneficial. A study followed children in grades one to three who went through a twelve-week program of breath awareness and yoga, which was delivered once a week every other week. The findings showed that the students who went through the program showed an increase in attentiveness, improvements in social skills, and a decrease in test anxiety when compared to students who did not have the training.[vii]

UCLA's Mindful Awareness Research Center conducted two pilot studies that followed preschool and elementary students who went through an eight-week mindful awareness practices training program for two thirty-minute sessions each week. Their findings showed improvements in self-regulatory abilities of the children who went through the training when compared to students who did not receive training. These studies show that practicing mindfulness in a school setting can have benefits for students.[viii]


## Other Benefits of Mindfulness

In a 2013 Massachusetts General Hospital Study, researchers found that mindfulness can reduce anxiety. They followed ninety-three people with a diagnosis of generalized anxiety disorder who underwent a mindfulness-based stress reduction group intervention for eight weeks. These participants showed a marked drop in their anxiety levels, which was much greater than the people who simply went through stress management education.[ix]

Mindfulness meditation was found to reduce age and race bias in a 2015 Central Michigan study. The participants were given either a mindfulness or a control audio to listen to. Those who listened to the mindfulness audio showed a drop in their implicit age and race bias as opposed to the group who did not. The professor who led this study revisited it again later, asking the participants to play a trust game where they were asked to look at pictures of people from different races and identify who they would trust to help them win money and who they would expect would steal money just by looking at the pictures. The people in the mindfulness group trusted people from both racial groups almost equally, while those in the other group selected the white people in the pictures as trustworthy much more often than the black people.[x]

A study conducted by researchers Ellen R. Albertson, Kristin D. Neff, and Karen E. Dill-Shackleford found that mindfulness can increase body satisfaction in women. In their study, those who underwent a three-week self-compassion meditation training showed more gains in self-compassion and body appreciation and a reduction in body shame and the feelings that their self-worth should be based on their appearance compared to the group who did not. These effects were even found to still be present even three months later.[xi]

A 2010 study published in the *Consciousness and Cognition Journal* found that cognitive abilities can be improved after even a short period of mindfulness training. Half of the participants in the study went through four days of mindfulness training while half of them listened to an audio book during the same time. Those who went through the mindfulness training reported less anxiety and fatigue and showed a more marked improvement in their visual-spatial processing skills and memory than those who did not.[xii]

## The Purpose of This Book

Through writing this book, it is my hope that I can help you to become more aware of your unconscious — often negative — mental chatter and seize control of it. I can't promise you that you will be able to stop it completely, as that's unnatural and I would never promise you such a lie. But by becoming aware of these negative thoughts, you can face them head-on as the outdated and often irrational fears that they are.

If you truly commit to becoming more mindful with everything in you, the exercises presented in this book won't be hard to follow. It is only when you wish to change and really get serious about taking action on it that it will happen for you. Let's get started!

Chapter 2 - Meditation

Have you ever wanted to try meditation, but were convinced you would never be any good at it? Have you found yourself watching meditation videos on YouTube or checking out Pinterest, only to feel doubtful that you could possibly compete with what you see? Well, fortunately for all of us, meditation is not a competition. Meditation is simply the act of calming and silencing the mind so that you can feel a sense of peace and be mindful in the present. Meditation can be done by anyone, anytime, and anywhere. This chapter will break down the process of meditation into simple, manageable steps and have you feeling inspired to make it a part of your life.

I am a Pinterest addict — don't laugh. Who's to say men can't be? I could spend hours on end searching for healthy recipes and countless other topics that I never even knew I was interested in. I love to cook, and am actually known for throwing together some pretty decent meals in my circle of family and friends. I am constantly looking to Pinterest for inspiration for new dishes to make. Unfortunately, this website that can bring me great joy can also at times become the bane of my existence.

When I find a recipe that looks intriguing to me, I end up taking one of two paths. I either become obsessed with matching every ingredient exactly and trying to make my food look even more beautiful than the picture they posted, which I am convinced is humanly impossible, or I relax and decide to make it my own. When I put a lot of pressure on myself, I take all of the joy out of preparing the food, and what is the point of cooking if you can't enjoy making meals for those you love? When I relax and decide that I'm going to make the recipe my own and just see how it turns out, it is a much more enjoyable experience, and often the result is better than I could ever have expected.

Meditation is sometimes like my Pinterest addiction. People often approach meditation with preconceived notions that stand in the way of them getting the most out of the experience. Many people have specific goals for the outcome of their meditation session: relieving stress, improving memory and focus, losing weight, etc. While meditation may ultimately help with all of these things and many more, by treating our meditation sessions as a goal rather than simply an intention, we are inadvertently putting undue pressure on ourselves. This can take us out of the moment and set us up for judging ourselves and experiencing a sense of disappointment if our goals are not met as quickly as we would like.

If we can overcome this and just set the intention of meditating in order to be mindful, we take away the pressure and judgment and can simply meditate for its own sake. We can decide to practice and see how it turns out. When we are able to just relax, we can truly start to quiet our minds and be present in the moment, and create a much more enjoyable, and eventually productive, experience.

## How to Meditate

There are many different techniques for meditation. The best part is that there is no one right or wrong way to do it. There is no one-size-fits-all method. You can rest assured that when you find a technique that helps you focus on just being mindful and in the moment, you have found a perfect technique for you. It doesn't matter whether it is yoga, saying a mantra, chanting, counting your breaths, or any of countless other methods. As long as it works for you, it is absolutely right.

I was a teacher for many years. While I appreciated questions that often had many right answers or countless ways to approach solving a problem, my students often did not. They wanted to be told what to do and usually saw things in black and white instead of infinite shades of gray. Since that was my life experience, I can understand that people who are new to meditation may appreciate some added guidance at first. While I can't tell you that there is only one correct technique, I can give you a sort of basic framework to get you started.

First, let's talk about our breathing and posture. Start by setting aside 10 to 15 minutes where you can go into a quiet room without distractions. If you find that this is too much time for you initially, you could start with a smaller amount of time and gradually increase it, or you could set a timer to help you stick with it.

Place a pillow on the floor and sit on it as you cross your legs sort of like a pretzel. If this is a difficult position for you, just do the best that you can while still being comfortable. No one is judging you here. Make sure your back is straight, but relax your abdomen and let your belly stick out. Look straight ahead and decide if having your eyes open or closed feels best to you. Put your hands on your knees or in your lap with your palms up.

Now that you are physically ready to meditate, let's work on getting mentally prepared. This may prove to be the hardest part. Quiet your mind and try to think about nothing at all. Breathe in through your nose and try to fill up your chest with air while your stomach pushes out a bit. Slowly exhale and count your breaths each time as you repeat the process over and over.

If you find thoughts or distractions creeping into your mind, start your counting over again at one. These thoughts will enter your mind, and as a beginner to meditation, you may not even immediately realize it when they do. Try not to get frustrated with yourself and want to give up. Just recognize that a thought has entered your mind, let go of it, and restart your counting. It is perfectly normal and fine if you don't get to count past two or three when you first start your mediation journey. Many people have to meditate for months before they are able to count all the way to 10.

The steps outlined above are a very basic type of Zen meditation, and hopefully after your meditation sessions, you will start to feel calmer, more relaxed, and focused as you continue with your daily activities.[xiii]

## **Benefits to Meditation**

As a busy husband and father of two kids, I consider having 10 to 15 minutes of quiet time to myself each day where I don't have to think about anything to be more than enough of a reward for meditating, but you may be wondering about what other benefits your meditation sessions may help you to achieve. There have been many studies conducted to research the positive results people can get from meditation.

A notable study was recently published in the journal *Psychological Science,* which sought to find brain functions that are improved by meditating. The study, led by Katherine MacLean from the University of California — Davis and authored by thirteen additional researchers, found that people who participate in intensive meditation are able to focus their attention and maintain it even during tasks which are considered very boring. The study participants who meditated regularly showed a greater focus, concentration, and attention to detail than their counterparts who did not mediate. The study also found that as people meditated more and improved in their meditation skills, these areas showed an even greater improvement over time.[xiv]

A significant number of other studies have also identified many benefits to meditation beyond improved focus and concentration. People who meditate have often been found to exhibit improved physical health. Meditation has been shown to help improve cardiovascular and immune health, aid in weight loss, help to curb addictions, lower cholesterol, increase energy levels, slow signs of aging, improve circulation, reduce stress, and help to relieve pain for many people. Meditation is a gift we can give ourselves, and it contributes to an overall feeling of wellness by encouraging a healthy lifestyle.


## Meditation and Daily Life

As I reflect on the value of meditation in my own life, and how by practicing it I am choosing to be mindful and present in the moment as I calm and quiet my mind and bring a sense of peace to my days, I am reminded of how this can impact every area of my life, especially the most important one to me — fatherhood. I think back over the years as I've watched my children grow. I can't believe how quickly time has gone by. It makes me yearn for a slower-paced life where I can take the time to cherish and enjoy the little moments in my children's lives. I am sure most other parents can relate to this feeling as well.

I think of all the time that passed by in what seems like the blink of an eye. The memories that seem to be more fleeting than I would like... It is in those moments that I was not being mindful and truly present. Those are the times when I was reading emails from work, surfing the internet, or trying to listen to something on television while I was only half-listening to my kids as they shared what happened during their day with exuberant joy. Those are the times when I was watching their sporting event or activity and thinking of all of the things I had to get done the next day at work. Those are the times when cooking dinner was more of my focus than the little ones asking me to play a game or read them a story. Those were the times when I was trying to juggle too much instead of being mindful and present. Those were the times when I missed out on precious moments and memories I can't get back.

Then there are those beautiful memories of family time, which I can replay in my mind with brilliant, vivid detail. They might have happened long ago, but I can relive them like they were just yesterday down to every last minute. The sights, sounds, and even smells are embedded in my mind for eternity. Those are the times when I was focused and attentive only to what was happening in the present. Those are the times when I silenced any other distractions from my mind and truly lived in the moment. Those are the times that I chose to be mindful. Those are the times that I cherish and have enjoyed the most in my life. I would hazard a guess that my children would remember most of those times as well, because they know when I am present in the time I spend with them and when I am not.

I now know that I do not have to wait and wish for a slower-paced life; I can choose to create it for myself. I can choose to be mindful and focused. I can choose to live in the present and silence the distractions that creep into my mind and threaten to steal my cherished memories. I can achieve that wish through meditation. The best thing of all is that everyone can. Meditation does not require one perfect technique or a set of special skills. Meditation can be done by anyone, anytime, anywhere. Just make a commitment to yourself and improving your well-being. Find a quiet room, devote a few minutes to thinking of absolutely nothing else, and just breathe. You might find that it can make a world of difference in your life. I know it has in mine.

## Chapter 3 – Spartan Discipline And Willpower

Do you have a big dream for yourself, one where you have plans, ideas, and goals for your future? One where you can picture your life filled with happiness, good health, and success? Of course, we all do! But a dream will stay a dream unless you have the self-discipline to stay focused and do the things you need to do to achieve your goal.

Whether you are trying to stop procrastinating and complete a big project at work, looking for the motivation to get up off the couch and stop making excuses about why you can't work out, or deciding now is the time to finally do something for yourself like writing the book you have always wanted to write, you won't be able to reach any of your goals without self-discipline. Self-discipline requires a conscious focus and awareness. What can make you more aware? Mindfulness.

## How to Acquire Discipline and Willpower

Not everything we do in our lives will be filled with sunshine and roses. There will be times when we have no other choice than to just grind through our work and put one foot in front of the other until it is done, no matter how miserable it may make us at the time. That's where discipline and willpower come in. They will help you to get through almost anything. If you find that you are lacking focus or motivation, discipline and willpower might be all you need to carry you through until you can find your center again.

Often, people think that they must rely on motivation or inspiration to create something or do their work. This is a false line of thought that usually causes people to sit around and wait for something to happen, while it rarely, if ever, does. If you are waiting for motivation or inspiration to strike you, you are relying on external things and giving away your power. The one thing you can rely on in life is yourself. It is your mental fortitude, self-discipline, and willpower that will get you where you need to go if you let them. No waiting needed.

As a writer, it can be easy to stare at a blank page and wait for the perfect moment of creative genius to come to you. I've found myself doing this on more than one occasion. Then I realized the more I stared at that blank page, the more power I gave it. I want my power to come from within myself, and I certainly don't want to give it away and give into a feeling of helplessness. I am sure that writers waiting for the perfect inspiration are why countless amazing books remain unwritten. I now choose to look at my blank page as a detour sign. I am no longer content to sit and wait for that divine inspiration to come to me. I choose to look for a path around it. It may mean that I skip that chapter for a while and work on another one, or that I write the conclusion to my book and work backwards, or maybe I settle for an imperfect chapter for the moment, knowing that I can always come back to it later and improve it when I make my revisions. Whatever path I choose to take, I don't stop moving. I keep putting one foot in front of the other and stay focused on my goal. My detour may have taken me off the original path I had in mind, but it is often the scenic routes in life which can offer us the best rewards.

## Self-Discipline, Willpower, and Delayed Gratification

Out of all of the things in life that could offer great insight into the human experience, I must admit that marshmallows are one of the last things I would expect. Walter Mischel, PhD, a psychologist who is now at Columbia University, proved that my doubt of the influence of a marshmallow was very misguided.

He created a simple test of self-control in children which came to be known as the "marshmallow test" and created the foundation for future studies of self-control. In his test, preschool children were given a plate of marshmallows and were told that the researcher needed to leave the room for a few minutes. The children were given a choice: If they did not touch the marshmallows until the researcher came back, they would be allowed to eat two marshmallows. If they decided they didn't want to wait, they could ring a bell and the researcher would come back right away, but they would only get to eat one marshmallow. This was testing the children's willpower, which can also be looked at as the ability to delay gratification.[xv]

Mischel revisited the participants in his study when they became teenagers to see if their choices as preschoolers could be indicative of something more impactful later in their lives. He found that the teenagers who had chosen to wait to eat the marshmallows when they were in preschool were more likely to receive better scores on their SATs later in life. Their parents also reported that they were better at planning, dealing with stress, showing self-control when they felt frustrated, and concentrating without getting distracted.

The marshmallow test was then revisited when B.J. Casey, PhD, of Weill Cornell Medical College along with Mischel, Yuichi Soda, PhD of the University of Washington, and other colleagues checked in with fifty-nine of the participants who are now in their 40s. This time, the researchers gave them a new test of their willpower by presenting them with a laboratory task which assessed self-control in adults. They found that the original results of the marshmallow test were still very accurate, even after all those years. The children who couldn't resist the temptation of the marshmallows were largely now adults who did poorly on the self-control task as well.

## Discipline is Inherently Hard

Oddly enough, we often see our future self as another person, which can contribute to our difficulty in being self-disciplined as we try to achieve our goals. Science even backs this up. In one study, researchers asked the participants to think about their current self, to think about a celebrity (Natalie Portman or Matt Damon), and to think about themselves in 10 years. They scanned the participants' brains as they did their thinking and found that the scans were almost exactly the same when they thought about their future selves as when they thought about the celebrity (a stranger).

Jason Mitchell from Harvard also found that when people imagine themselves experiencing something enjoyable a year from now, many people use the same brain areas that they do when they think of a stranger.[xvi]

This may help us to understand why people may be willing to behave in self-destructive ways in the present while giving little thought to the consequences those actions may have for their lives in the future. This brings to mind all of the warnings we try to give to young adults that their social media posts and online interactions now can have a big impact on their lives later on when their future employers look at their behavior. All too often, they experience a disconnect between their present and future selves and lack self-discipline. Our warnings go unheeded, leading to difficult consequences.

## Scientific Methods to Increase Discipline

A joint study was conducted at the Hong Kong University of Science and the University of Chicago, which found that if students were asked to remember a time when they resisted temptation, 70% of them indulged in temptation at their next opportunity. But if the question was changed to ask them to remember why they resisted temptation, 69% of the students resisted the temptation. This seems to suggest that one way to improve your self-discipline is to remind yourself of the reason you want to resist giving in.[xvii]

Another study gave some hope to many who struggle to find the self-discipline needed to resist the temptation to use drugs. It found that adults who were recovering from drug abuse had reduced cravings and depression after they participated in deliberate, slow breathing for 20 minutes. We can certainly apply this technique to give our self-discipline a boost in many other areas of our lives as well.

Northwestern University conducted a study of 40 adults in romantic relationships by separating them into three groups. The first group was encouraged to use their non-dominant hand when they brushed their teeth. The second group was encouraged to start saying "yes" instead of "yeah." The third group acted as the control group and wasn't given any instruction at all.

After two weeks of participation, the first two groups displayed fewer tendencies to get angry or violent with their romantic partners, while the third group exhibited no change in this behavior. While there doesn't seem to be a natural connection between what they were asked to do and the ultimate results, by simply being more conscious and aware in even one area of their lives, there was an impact in other areas as well. It may seem like a small thing, but being mindful forced their brains to pause and make a choice to do the harder thing instead of the easier one. In this case, their brains paused and decided to stay calm (harder) rather than reacting with anger to something that upset them (easier).[xviii]

When we choose to be mindful, we are making the conscious choice to be aware and present in the moment. We are choosing to be focused. Being mindful is a way of life. It helps us to reach our goals and dreams by increasing our self-discipline. Without self-discipline and willpower, our dreams are little more than a wish and we are no closer to achieving them. We are the only ones we can rely upon to create the lives we want for ourselves, not some external source of inspiration and motivation. Our power must come from within ourselves. Mindfulness offers us the vehicle to get us where we want to go. Meditation is the gasoline which powers that vehicle.

Chapter 4 – Befriend Yourself

**Turn Your Volume Down**

As we have learned from numerous studies discussed in the previous chapter, mindfulness meditation can enhance our cognitive abilities, improve the speed and depth of what we are able to remember, and help us to better incorporate new knowledge into our brains. Another study published in the journal *Brain Research Bulletin* may help to explain why.

Have you ever had to tell your child to turn down their music, television, or video game because it was so loud that you couldn't even hear yourself think? Well, that is sort of how our brain works as well. Our brain cells use waves which help to control the information that enters our brain. There is a key brain wave called the alpha rhythm that acts as sort of the volume switch on our brain. It is very active in the areas of our brains that receive information from our senses and send that information to other parts of the brain. It has the power to "turn down the volume" on distractions as they try to enter our consciousness so we can focus on the important things.

Through mindful meditation, we are able to bring attention to our senses, feelings, and state of mind so we turn up the volume on those areas that we are focused on and turn down the volume of the distractions that are bringing in information that we don't need. This allows our brain to work at a more efficient and higher-functioning level, and we are able to improve our ability to quickly remember things and to incorporate new knowledge.[xix]

The idea of mindfulness meditation being able to control the volume of what enters our brain and turn down distractions takes me back to my childhood memories of playing sports. Talk about an overwhelming and overstimulating setting! You have the fans and coaches for both teams yelling, an announcer talking over the loudspeaker, cheerleaders, referees, whistles, buzzers, lights, cameras, the weather conditions, perhaps your opponents talking trash to psych you out, teammates, and your own mental chatter all entering your head at once. That's a lot to take in! While I didn't know about mindfulness meditation at that point in my life, it sure would have come in handy!

One of the first things I did at the beginning of any of my sporting events was locate my parents in the stands. Seeing them always brought me a sense of comfort as I knew that no matter what happened or how I played, they were the two people who would always be on my side. Then I put on the headphones of my Walkman for a few minutes, not to listen to the music really, but just to help me tune everything else out. During the game, I somehow was always able to hear my dad yelling encouragement from the stands. I am sure his voice wasn't the loudest in the crowd, but my mind was always able to turn his volume up and the volume of everything else down. Maybe I was doing my own version of mindfulness meditation even then. It sure helped me when I played sports, so I am grateful for it.

**Don't Take Your Thoughts Personally**

There is a line of thought that may help us to keep the negative thoughts that creep into our minds in a better perspective. We learned earlier that up to 80% of the daily thoughts of an average person can be negative thoughts, so it is very easy to be hard on ourselves and let that negative mental chatter weigh us down, which keeps us from being our best selves and finding happiness.

Rev. Nancy Colier, a licensed clinical social worker and psychotherapist, points out that everyone lives in their own small, internal world. We have thoughts that pop into our minds without us even realizing how they got there. In our minds, we think our thoughts are what others are thinking too, but in reality, there is no way for anyone else to know what we are thinking unless we share it with them. In fact, these thoughts will simply go away and disappear if we don't focus on them. We give them energy and staying power when we dwell on them. If we turn down the volume on those negative thoughts and stop feeding them, they will go away. We might find that we can focus on more positive thoughts and be a little kinder to ourselves in the process.[xx]

Mark Manson, a bestselling author, thinker, and life enthusiast, offers yet another perspective on why we shouldn't get bogged down by our negative thoughts. He says that everyone in the history of the world has been wrong about pretty much everything, so why should we profess that we are right about anything with absolute certainty? Manson concludes that instead of searching life for ultimate truths and believing that our own opinions are better than anyone else's, we should just accept the fact that, at best, we are only partially right. Our goal should be to learn, grow, and improve ourselves so that tomorrow, we can be less wrong than we are today.[xxi]

As a teacher, and one who is fascinated by studying history, I love that line of thinking. We should absolutely strive to be lifelong learners and be willing to change our perceptions and opinions when we are presented with information that disputes what we previously believed to be true. It reminds me of something my grandmother used to say: *"I did the best I could, and when I knew better, I did better."* If we consider ourselves to be works in progress, we can take away some of the undue pressure and judgments we make about ourselves and just work to grow and improve. Quieting the negative thoughts in our minds just might be a nice place to start.

## Proprioception and Interoception

The medical definition of proprioception is "the ability to sense stimuli arising within the body regarding position, motion, and equilibrium. Even if a person is blindfolded, he or she knows through proprioception if an arm is above the head or hanging by the side of the body." So you might be wondering what proprioception has to do with mindfulness.

We experience so many things in our lives through our senses (our body), and we may be completely unaware of that fact. We are usually so wrapped up in paying attention to other things that we often miss out on all that our senses contribute to our lives. We can do a lot to change that! When we practice mindfulness through yoga or other techniques, we get connected to our bodies and all of their parts as we get to know ourselves better from the inside out.

Great thinkers, like Buddha, know the importance of our physical senses. He believed that "physical sensations are the first foundation of mindfulness because they are intrinsic to feelings and thoughts and are the base of the very process of consciousness." Obviously, being connected as one with our bodies is crucial in achieving mindfulness, but there are some obstacles that get in our way.

Our bodies require so much thought and energy to work properly that if we had to constantly think about taking a breath or making our heart beat, we wouldn't be able to survive. That is why as a survival mechanism the body has to make the muscles that we use all of the time "unconscious muscles," and they can act without us really having to think about them. The problem is that these unconscious muscles often leave our awareness, which is a barrier to true mindfulness.

Yoga works to bring these "forgotten" muscles back into our awareness by performing asana and putting new demands on the body and brain. This creates a sort of "reunited and it feels so good" feeling when you practice mindfulness meditation and yoga; your mind and body are once again united and running at their full potential.

Proprioception is vital to keeping us safe as we age too. We can unfortunately lose the body-mind connection if we don't stay physically active. One of the biggest dangers for senior citizens is falling, which can cause serious injury and even death. Falling becomes more common in the elderly population because our proprioception gradually becomes weaker over time if we are unable to maintain physical activity in our lives.

Proprioception is so critical to our well-being because we need to be aware of the position of all of the parts of our bodies, even when we can't see them. We depend on this to be able to walk through a dark room without losing our balance and falling, to be able to keep our eyes on the road as we drive instead of watching our hands and feet to see what they are doing to operate the car, to be able to do so many things in our daily lives that we take for granted and don't fully appreciate.

Sometimes in our fast-paced and busy lives, we spend so much time in our heads that we can feel very disconnected from our bodies. Practicing yoga and mindfulness is one way we can reconnect and find our center again. That is where we can strengthen our proprioception on a regular basis until we trust our bodies to be there for us and we really know ourselves inside and out. Once we trust our bodies, we can begin to trust our hearts too. We can listen to our guiding inner voice and be confident it won't steer us wrong.

Interoception is a lesser-known, but no less important skill to have. There are receptors inside all of our organs that gather information about what is going on inside our bodies and send that information to our brain. This helps us to be aware of our body temperature, heart and breathing rate, hunger, thirst and many other bodily functions. Interoception makes us aware of what is happening in our bodies so that we can make the adjustments we need to make to help ourselves. It tells us when we need to eat and drink, when we need to slow down because our heart is beating too fast, when we are too cold or too hot and need to do something about it, and so many other things vital to our physical well-being.[xxii]

In order to improve our interoception, we need to let go of any preconceived notions about what we will or should feel, be aware of our body's physical sensations without becoming fixated on any individual sensation for too long, and turn down the volume on our mental chatter so we can be mindful and pay attention to what our bodies are telling us.

Sometimes people think they know and can predict their pain so accurately that it sort of becomes a self-fulfilling prophecy. They become so confident that they know exactly how their bodies are going to feel that they often don't realize if their expectations are wrong and their pain is less than they feared it would be. Interoception requires people to let go of those expectations and just be mindful and truly aware of what is actually happening inside their bodies at any given moment.

Interoception can improve our body-mind connection if we let go of our predictions and expectations and look at the pain we experience through neutral eyes that don't make judgements, but rather look gently upon the pain we may feel and try to make the adjustments we can to lessen it. Practicing mindfulness can strengthen our interoception.

Neuroscientists are studying the positive effects that being interoceptively aware can have on our brains, immune systems, and emotions. A strong and healthy interoception is key to our physical, mental, and emotional well-being.

## Chapter 5 – Do Nothing

Do nothing and accomplish everything!

This sounds like a dream come true for every frazzled, exhausted, overwhelmed, and overworked man and woman I have ever met in my life. It also sounds like every warning anyone ever gave me. I can practically hear my parents telling me, "If it sounds too good to be true, it probably is."

Thankfully it is not the tale spun by a slick salesman, but rather a different perspective and way of viewing the world called *wu-wei*, offered by Lao Tzu, a revered ancient Chinese writer and philosopher who became the father of Taoism.

## What Does "Do Nothing" or "Non-Doing" Mean?

Wu-wei is the art of non-doing. In our frenetic society, wu-wei seems to go against everything we have been taught is important. Our society places great value on getting things done and staying busy all of the time. From an early age, we are taught that this is the way to get ahead. We must work hard all the time and get things accomplished in order to be successful in life.

Wu-wei does not promote laziness or sitting back and watching life pass us by, but it is a sort of paradigm shift that teaches us to "work smarter, not harder." Non-doing is not really doing nothing; it is just removing our own self-imposed desires and attempts to control every situation, and instead opening ourselves up to acting only in the ways that nature requires, sort of going with the flow instead of fighting against it.[xxiii]

When our human nature kicks in and tries to take control, we often get in our own way and make things worse. We can become nervous, frustrated, stressed, and impatient when things don't go the way we think they should. Then we enter a cycle where we overdo things. We try too hard and often end up doing more, but achieving less than we could have if we would have just let go of our preconceived notions of how things should be and accept things for how they are. Instead of wasting our time and energy worrying about why things aren't as we think they should be, we could follow the natural order of things and be more effective and efficient with our time, thus getting more done with less effort and struggle.

## The Benefits of Wu-Wei

Have you ever had a day that you felt like you were working very hard to get things done, but you were going in circles or walking in quicksand and not really accomplishing anything? When you felt like you didn't have a moment to spare, yet when you finally gave in and sat down for five minutes to breathe or stopped long enough to take a 20-minute nap, you had a whole new perspective and got a lot more done afterwards? Maybe you, like me, have misplaced something like your keys and frantically ran around your house looking for them, getting more and more frustrated by the moment. It may only be when you stop looking that you are able to find them. For me, it is usually only after I pause to quiet my mind and gather my composure that a thought pops into my head, reminding me of the last place I left them. Perhaps you have wanted something so badly, like a new job, where you ended up putting so much pressure on yourself that you couldn't be your best self in interviews and let potential employers see the real you living up to your full potential.

All of these are examples of how we try to impose our will on situations instead of just going with the flow and following the natural order of things. They all show us how doing more does not always mean getting more accomplished. It is when we take the time to slow down and accept things as they are that we are non-doing and are often able to get more done.

By practicing wu-wei, we are letting things happen naturally and letting nature take its course. Lao Tzu said, "If you are depressed, you live in the past. If you are anxious, you live in the future. But if you are at peace, you are in the present." Practicing wu-wei can take the stress, worry, and feelings of disappointment out of our bodies and simply let us exist in harmony with nature. This definitely contributes to our physical, mental, and emotional well-being.

Wu-wei allows us to be more productive, efficient, and effective in the use of our time and energy. It allows us to accomplish more while trying less. We can expend less effort and energy. We might feel as though we have discovered more time in our day when we let things happen in their own time instead of imposing our artificial time tables on them. Focusing on our relationships can be more of a priority.

Physically, we may find that we have less headaches and stomach ailments, lower blood pressure, a stronger immune system, and our hearts and lungs do not have to work as hard on a daily basis. We may have less feelings of depression and anxiety, and we may be able to sleep better without the constant pressure from the mental chatter in our heads telling us of all the things we have to get done in a very short amount of time.

## How You Can Begin to Practice Wu-wei

If you have already begun your meditation journey, you are already on your way to practicing wu-wei. Meditation involves quieting the mind and letting it be unoccupied by other thoughts and distractions as you live in the moment and are mindful and aware of what is happening within and around you. Wu-wei takes the principle of mindful meditation a step farther. Anyone can start to practice wu-wei today with just a few simple steps.

First, take the opportunity to spend time in nature. Don't just pass through it. Stop and take the time to really experience it. Quietly observe it. Just be still and become connected to it. This will be your first step in being able to go with the natural flow of life instead of imposing your own will and fighting against it.[xxiv]

Next, take a lesson from the natural world. Go against the grain of human nature, which assumes that scarcity is the norm. We often are hesitant to give to and share with others based on the fear that if we do, we may not have enough for ourselves. Nature acts in the opposite way, being very giving and generous. The sun gives us all of its light and heat without running out or becoming depleted. From seeds grow fruit. The fruit is food to many living creatures, and the fruit also produces many seeds which allows many more animals to be fed in the future. In times of hurricanes, the gopher tortoise opens its burrow home to other species as a refuge, including some animals which may typically be a threat to them. A burrow may serve as a home or refuge to 350-400 other species. They are all able to peacefully co-exist and share a living space without fear of harm. We can certainly learn to be more generous by taking our cues from nature. In doing so, we bring ourselves closer to the natural flow of things and become more connected to nature. We may even find that through giving, we come to receive more than we could ever have thought possible.

The next step toward joining the natural flow of the universe is to let go of our fixed notions of what our lives should look like. We sometimes become so fixated on our expectations of how things should be that we close ourselves off to new possibilities. If we can let go of these preconceived ideas, we can open ourselves up to accepting things as they really are. This brings us ever closer to the natural flow of life.

Wu-wei believes that natural flow is not planned, but instead occurs spontaneously. Being open to that spontaneity and all that it has to offer is how we become more connected to the natural flow. A farmer can do everything humanly possible to prepare for a good harvest — till the soil, fertilize and irrigate, carefully plant seeds for optimum performance and growth, and protect against pests and disease — but he or she can't predict and guarantee the outcome with any certainty. That is where being open to spontaneity comes in. Our lives are very similar. There are limits to what we can do on our own. We just have to let go of control and be open to spontaneous opportunities.

Taking these four small steps will have you on your way to practicing wu-wei and uncovering the power of non-doing in your daily life. Just open yourself up to doing less and accomplishing more, and you may be surprised at the results you can achieve.

Chapter 6- Mindfulness and Goal Setting

Goal setting is a buzzword in today's society. We have it drilled into our heads on a regular basis that we must have clear goals for ourselves and follow our plans faithfully if we want to be successful in life. However, since practicing mindful meditation is all about living in the present and goals are all about making a plan for the future, you may wonder if it is possible for mindfulness and goal setting to harmoniously co-exist, or if they are destined to be at odds with one another.

## Can Mindfulness and Goal Setting Co-Exist?

Mindfulness does not require the absence of goals. On the contrary, goals are a necessary part of spiritual growth. If goals are set with a proper objective and followed in the appropriate way, they are a huge asset to us in our quest for mindfulness. We just need to be aware of some of the problems goals can cause us as we practice mindfulness and shift our thinking to make the necessary adjustments to our goals. It is then that mindfulness and goal setting can live in peaceful harmony.

## Common Mistakes People Make When Setting Goals

Goal setting is not as easy as it may seem. There are many pitfalls and mistakes that people make when they set their goals, which could get in the way of them achieving mindfulness.

Sometimes we cling to our goals at all costs and can be hard on ourselves when we don't meet them. And once we get even a small taste of success, we can become so consumed and desperate to try to repeat that exact experience that we become frustrated and distracted. Thoughts of self-doubt and criticizing ourselves can easily start to creep into our minds.

So how do we solve the problem of clinging onto and grasping after our goals? We need to stop holding our goals as expectations in our minds and getting mad at ourselves and feeling defeated when we don't reach them. Instead, we should hold onto them lightly and look at our goals as a sort of compass that points us in the direction we want to go. Goals can't be our obsession or seen as something we must achieve if we want to practice true mindfulness.

We need to accept that change isn't neat and clean and doesn't happen overnight. It will be unpredictable and have its ups and downs. We just need to be aware of and accept where we are now and use that as our starting point. We must accept the present moment for what it is. Acceptance is a necessary part of our growth. We aren't going to be instantly happy just because we set goals.

They say life is what happens when we are busy making other plans, so it is important that we aren't overly hard on ourselves when things don't turn out quite as we hope. We need to embrace the unpredictability of life and go with the flow. If we avoid the mistakes of taking our goals too seriously and not being flexible with them, we will be more in harmony with our mindfulness principles.

## Setting Good Goals for Ourselves

Setting inappropriate goals is another common mistake people make. Sometimes people set materialistic goals, mistakenly believing that they will make them happy. While there may be an initial uptick in happiness if one gains material wealth, the feeling is usually fleeting because it relies on an external source to generate our happiness.

True happiness comes from within and is created by our attitudes. Goals directed toward expressing gratitude for the things we have, appreciating our loved ones, showing empathy or patience toward others, or faithfully setting aside time to meditate can positively impact our attitudes in a major way and really contribute to our long-term happiness.

Mindfulness and goal setting do not need to be mutually exclusive, nor should they be. While it is true that mindfulness requires being in the present moment, it really means being able to silence the distractions that will take us out of the present by making us worry without even being truly aware of those thoughts. Being in the present moment simply means that we are aware of what we are doing right now.

It is possible to be mindful and still think of things that happened in the past, or may happen in the future, as long as we are aware of our thinking. When we are aware, we can make necessary adjustments to our thoughts and keep ourselves from being fixated on them. We can't do this when the thoughts pop up in our minds as distractions that we are all too often unaware of.

## A Brief Introduction to the Acceptance and Commitment Therapy

Acceptance and Commitment Therapy/Training (ACT) is often used in a workplace or psychotherapy setting. ACT takes the principles of mindfulness and puts them together with techniques designed to bring about a change in behavior or increased motivation. The goal of Acceptance and Commitment Therapy/Training is to help people accept the things that happen which are beyond their control and to stop the negative thoughts which all too often creep into our minds. By doing this, people are better equipped to deal with physical pain and feelings of failure while feeling less afraid of taking risks and facing uncertainty. ACT encourages people to become more active participants in their own lives and teaches them coping mechanisms for tolerating stress, allowing them to focus on the things in their lives that they can change and have power over.

## How Can ACT Help You Reach Your Goals?

Acceptance and Commitment Therapy/Training has been particularly helpful for people struggling with substance abuse problems, suffering with debilitating pain, or facing depression and anxiety, but that doesn't mean there aren't things that all of us can learn and benefit from as well. ACT has several guiding foundational principles which can help us with setting our personal goals.

Very much like mindfulness, ACT encourages people to be focused on living in the present, to face it head-on, and to tune out other things that may serve as distractions. It stresses that our feelings are a snapshot of where we were in a given moment in time, and we are capable of experiencing them and then releasing them and moving forward. We are not forever tied to our feelings and they do not define us, just as we should not attempt to cling too tightly to our goals to the point where we may be hard on ourselves if we don't achieve them.

As we learned earlier in this chapter, acceptance is a crucial ingredient in our spiritual growth and is connected to goal setting. ACT subscribes to this principle as well. It encourages people to accept their current life situation for what it is and be willing to experience it, even if it is not the place they would have liked to be in if they were given a choice. This also relates to our being able to release our preconceived notions when we set our goals. Acceptance and Commitment Therapy/Training also focuses on making a commitment to doing things a little at a time to make yourself healthier and happier.

ACT uses mindfulness and other exercises to help people to be aware of their thoughts and feelings. It stresses for us to recognize that our thoughts and feelings are just a glimpse into how we are experiencing life at a given moment in time, sort of a snapshot, which can reveal important information to us, but does not need to be held onto and fixated on. Our thoughts and feelings do not need to define us. We are still capable of making our own choices of our own free will. We are able to choose how much focus and weight we give to a certain thought or feeling and we are able to decide if we want to just let it go and move past it. This is very similar to the idea that we should just loosely hold onto our goals and treat them as a sort of compass for the direction we would like our lives to take.

Acceptance and Commitment Therapy/Training helps people who have often lost their center and guiding light because they have become distracted and focused on other difficulties in their lives. It acts as sort of a reset button, attempting to get them to reconnect with their own core values and get back on track with the people and things that mean the most to them and act as their personal guiding principles. This correlates with the notion of setting appropriate goals for ourselves which are more concerned with internal attitudes than external sources of happiness like wealth.

The final guiding principle of Acceptance and Commitment Therapy/Training involves being committed to take action. This principle is all about the importance of goal setting and the small steps that anyone can start to take to reach their goals. ACT focuses on not having specific expectations for how things will turn out in the end because it recognizes that there are many influences beyond a person's control at work.[xxv]

Setting goals is crucial for our personal and spiritual growth. If we set goals with proper objectives and follow them in appropriate ways, they can prove to be a great asset to us in our quest for mindfulness. It really is possible for goal setting and mindfulness to work hand in hand and help us to be our best selves.

# Chapter 7 – Energy Management With Mindfulness

Walking in quicksand... if you're a parent, you've been there and you'll understand exactly what I mean. Mornings in my house were frantic. My wife and I were raising our voices more often than we'd like as we tried to get our kids to hustle through the morning routine and humor us by getting everyone out the door at least somewhere close to on time. Everyone ended up stressed out and starting off their day on the wrong foot. I compare it to walking in quicksand because my wife and I were expending a great deal of energy and working quite hard to get everyone focused and cooperating, but we weren't experiencing the kind of success that we'd like. We ended up feeling exhausted and like we had not gotten as far as we had hoped. My wife and I decided something had to change for our sanity and the well-being of our family. We were working as hard as we could, but we weren't achieving the positive results we desired. We made up our minds that it was time for us to work smarter, not harder.

We began to look at our evening routine because that is a time that works well for our family. We always make it a point to sit down to dinner together as often as is humanly possible. It's our family commitment that the evening from dinner time on is family time. We do not allow electronics at the dinner table. Everyone plugs them in to the charging station and the kids may not access them after that point. If they need to work on a computer for homework, they use a laptop and their focus is their school work. During dinner, we each share things that happened in our day and talk about our plans for the next day. So it was a natural extension for us to take a few minutes after dinner to lay out our outfits and anything else that we would need in the morning and make it organized and easily accessible. We also relocated our charging station for the cell phones by the door to the garage. Now we just grab our phones as we walk out the door instead of getting distracted by them as we try to get ready. Those small changes made a big difference in making for pleasant, calm, efficient mornings for our whole family. We worked smarter, not harder and the payoff was huge.

Now think about your own life. When do you feel that you are under the most stress? If you are like the average person, it is probably when you feel like you are running out of time, and can't stay on schedule to finish what you started. There are countless self-help books and articles out there which try to offer you tips and techniques for successful time management. However, they may be leading you down a less productive path. Research now suggests that it is more important for us to focus on managing our energy rather than struggling to manage time which often proves elusive and, since it comes in a finite amount, is nearly impossible to truly manage. In our fast-paced busy lives it is natural to think that if we push ourselves harder we should be able to accomplish more, but it is impossible to be productive if we try to keep high energy levels all throughout our entire day. We simply can't function at an energy level 10 one hundred percent of the time. We need to work smarter, not harder.

When we allow ourselves to get stressed out because we feel like our time is running out, our ability to think clearly, and be mindful, decreases greatly. Through mindfulness, we can change our stress levels and productivity. If we focus on the things we can control, like managing our energy levels smartly, we will start to see an improvement in all aspects of our daily lives.

## The Science behind the Value of Mindfulness

We have discussed many times in this book the benefits of having a strong mind-body connection and how being mindful helps us to attain this invaluable connection. The scientific research backs this up as well. The Federal Aviation Administration conducted a study which found that taking short breaks during long working sessions caused a 16% improvement in focus and awareness.

Why is this? Taking breaks is actually following your body's natural rhythm. Nathaniel Kleitman, a physiologist and the sleep researcher who co-discovered REM sleep, is famous for finding that we alternate between light and deep sleep in 90 minute time periods. Kleitman also went on to find that our bodies follow the same 90 minute rhythm during the day as we move between periods of being more and less alert. According to Tony Schwartz, in his article in the Harvard Business Review, after people work very intensely for longer than 90 minutes, they begin to rely on stress hormones as their source of energy. He writes that the prefrontal cortex of the brain starts to shut down and people begin to struggle to think clearly.

Too often, people try to counteract these natural periods of low alertness by consuming caffeine or sugary foods. It is well known that any energy boost one receives from consuming these foods or drinks is short lived, so people may be better served by following their bodies' natural rhythm and taking short breaks to rest and regroup.

Research on ultradian rhythms conducted by Peretz Lavie agrees with these findings. When people work productively for 90 minutes and then take a short fifteen-twenty minute break, they are acting more in sync with their bodies' natural energy cycles and are able to stay focused and maintain higher energy levels throughout the day.

This cycle is being followed by people in all different professional fields. Some of the most talented violinists in the world share the common schedule of practicing their instrument intensely for 90 minutes and then taking a fifteen minute break. The U.S. Army Research Institute also conducted a study finding that people have better focus and increased levels of energy for longer amounts of time when they work for 90 minutes and then take a fifteen-twenty minute break.

Dr. Alejandro Lleras, a psychology professor at the University of Illinois, believes it is crucial for people to build in occasional breaks from work, regardless of how they decide to spend their few minutes of rest. A study was conducted on eighty-four subjects who were expected to perform a simple task on the computer for an hour. The people who were allowed to take two short breaks during that time had a consistent performance through the whole hour, while the people who weren't given a break had a decrease in performance over time. After our bodies and minds are exposed to stimulation constantly for an extended period of time, our brains begin to view the stimulus as being unimportant and our minds erase it from our awareness. Taking a break is imperative in order for our brain to view the stimulus as being new enough to allow us to focus on it again.

## Know Your Body Well

As we already discussed, a big part of being mindful means living in the present moment and being connected to our bodies. The better we are able to know ourselves and our bodies and how they are linked, the more productive we will be able to be in our daily lives. Most people have times of the day when they usually feel more mentally sharp and focused and have more physical energy. If we are able to plan our schedules around those peak performance periods, we may find that our days can be much more productive.

While not everyone's body has the exact same Circadian Rhythms of high and low function, there are often similar times of day for many people. It is common for many to find it hardest to concentrate and stay focused between the hours of twelve-four p.m. Studies have found that the brain is typically best at dealing with difficult cognitive tasks after ten a.m. once the body has been fed and the brain has had a chance to become fully awake. It may prove to be a good idea for people to focus their intense energy levels on the most difficult things they need to face in the late morning and then build in a break in the afternoon during the times of most distraction. Creative thinking has been shown to increase during the afternoon hours for many people, so allowing yourself some time to think about problems which may require some creativity to solve during that time period may prove to be productive.

While it would be nice if we could all wave a magic wand and make the stress in our lives disappear, unfortunately it is simply not possible to erase our stress. However, a well-balanced day is a part of living our lives with mindfulness. We can create focused lives for ourselves and choose to concentrate on the things we can control, like where and when to best spend our energy. By listening to our bodies and minds, we will find infinite ways to work smarter, not harder and reclaim some of the productivity we may have lost.

Chapter 8 – Mindfulness in Your Life Areas

Now that we have taken a closer look at what mindfulness is, it's time to put it into practice in our daily lives. In this chapter, we will see how to make mindfulness a part of three life areas: personal growth, relationships, and in the workplace.

**Personal Growth**

We all have an inner critic at work in our minds from time to time. You know, the one who is constantly in the back of your mind telling you that you aren't good enough, that you don't work hard enough, that you can't compare to others. This negative mental chatter never seems to go away, no matter how hard we work to better ourselves. We begin to feel exhausted and defeated as we realize we can never do enough or be enough to measure up to the unrealistic expectations our inner critic has set for us.

This inner critic issues judgments on us, which makes it different from mindfulness. When we are mindful, we know how to manage our time and be resourceful with what we have to help us grow and improve ourselves. When we have the inner critic at work judging us harshly, we always feel the need to get better, but we can't truly grow. The inner critic is never patient, allowing us to relax and enjoy life, or to even take the time for self-improvement. It is just demanding of us to meet its impossible expectations.

Mindfulness and self-improvement are forever intertwined. You can't have one without the other. Being truly mindful requires that you work on yourself. Improving yourself grows your mindfulness. Now we will discuss how to improve yourself through being mindful using five techniques that you should be able to practically implement in your daily life.

The first technique involves improving your breathing. Our judgmental inner critic causes tension in our bodies and minds. Meditation is one way to relieve that tension, but meditation takes a while to practice fully. One simple way to release tension in a matter of just a few minutes is by practicing your breathing. You can do this by inhaling deeply for five to 10 seconds, holding your breath for two to three seconds, and then exhaling for five to 10 seconds. In a very short amount of time, you will begin to feel a sense of calmness come over you.

The next technique is to remember your state of mind as you are breathing. As you breathe, think about nothing. Remember what this feels like and be able to do it again every time it feels like you are blaming yourself too much. Being calm is connected to being mindful. If you get to the point where you are good at being able to get yourself to calm down, then you will be better at getting yourself to be mindful.

Learning to grow your kindness is the next technique. When our inner critic is at work judging us, it is never nice. Being mindful makes you kind. When you are mindful, you are better at communicating with other people through kindness, and are ultimately able to listen to and learn from them as you try to better yourself. If you allow yourself to be stuck with your judgmental inner critic, you won't be able to listen to others, and you will miss out on all of the things you could have learned from them.

The fourth technique is to give more to others. If you take the time to share your knowledge and experience with others, you ultimately come to learn more about yourself. You look more carefully and deeply at yourself and your life, and you are able to decide what is truly important to you.

Finally, if you are going to be a mindful person, you have to be aware of your emotions. You need to be able to be calm, even as frustrations begin to arise. When things go wrong, you have to find your center and calm down as you start to analyze the problem. Being aware of and able to gain control over your negative thoughts and feelings is the best way to silence your inner critic and keep from being hard on yourself.

When we are trying to improve ourselves, setting goals is a natural extension of this. As we learned in our last chapter, we must be cautious and change our usual thinking of how we should set goals. We always have to be careful not to cling too much to our preconceived expectations and ideas to the point where we judge ourselves and allow that inner critic to gain too much power. If we allow ourselves to be so consumed with the thought that we should be somewhere else, it is possible that this can fill up our whole lives and still leave us unfulfilled.

## Mindfulness in Relationships

Can being mindful really help improve our relationships? Research supports this idea. In the February 2016 issue of the *Journal of Human Sciences and Extension,* a meta-analysis found that mindfulness is connected to greater relationship satisfaction. The study combined results from 12 studies and found that mindfulness has a reliable impact on relationship satisfaction.[xxvi]

As we discussed in earlier chapters, mindfulness can make people more empathetic and compassionate toward others, as well as less impulsive. It improves one's ability to respond to conflict more positively and not get overwhelmed by stress. There is a scientific reason for this.

The amygdala is what detects threats and sends signals of alarm to the brain. Mindfulness makes this part of the brain less powerful and improves the connection between the amygdala and the prefrontal cortex, which better equips people to calm themselves when they feel angry or afraid so they don't get bogged down by negativity. This can make people less likely to perceive the behavior of their partner as a threat to their well-being and happiness, and feel less of a need to protect themselves and be more willing to protect their relationship instead.

Mindfulness strengthens another area of the brain as well. The anterior cingulate cortex (ACC) is responsible for our self-perception and regulating our attention, impulses, and emotions. It is the part of the brain that also allows our thinking to be flexible enough that we can see things from perspectives other than our own. It gives us the ability to change instead of staying fixated on one negative view of ourselves or our partner.

The ACC can make it possible for us to be able to break away from past traumas and insecurities we may have that can negatively impact our relationships. Mindfulness can help us to calm ourselves so we aren't tempted to engage in negative behaviors like avoiding intimacy or controlling our partners. In essence, it makes us better equipped to grow and change in our relationships and within ourselves as we are faced with new obstacles throughout our lives.

Finally, mindfulness helps to change our insula for the better. The insula is the part of our brain connected to our empathy and emotional awareness. We become more aware of our own feelings as well as our partner's, allowing us to be more compassionate to both parties. Mindfulness allows us to be more accepting of our partners instead of being obsessed with what we perceive to be their flaws. We start to see them in a more positive light. We begin to understand that their behavior is related to their life experiences and are more likely to be understanding and forgiving. Being more aware of our feelings makes us less likely to overreact to stressful triggers and allow them to negatively impact our relationships.

Mindfulness is a great asset to us in our quest for better relationships. By allowing us to be more present and attentive to our partners, we are better able to be intimate and loving and have happier and more connected relationships. We are less likely to argue with our partners over every little thing and become emotionally distant. We can recognize when we are starting to behave in unhelpful or unhealthy ways and change before things get out of hand. Mindfulness allows us to be warmer and more loving partners which creates better relationships for everyone involved.

## Mindfulness at Work

Our workplaces are often filled with stress and competitiveness as we strive for promotions and raises. As we know, this can be a slippery slope if we are not equipped to deal with stress without simply reverting to our brain's autopilot responses, or if we do not shift our thinking to creating better and healthier goals for ourselves. Mindfulness increases our awareness of these negative and often destructive patterns we all too often fall into, and allows us to change our thinking and responses before negativity takes root and causes irreparable damage to our workplace relationships.

In an article for Forbes, Drew Hansen notes that our minds will wander and we should not try to force it not to.[xxvii] Instead, through mindfulness meditation, we should just train our brain to take notice of where it wanders and then return the focus of our attention back to our breathing. The goal should not be to keep our mind from wandering, but rather to be able to bring our thoughts back to the present when it does. This will help us to stay centered in the present at work and make us less likely to react in negative and unproductive ways.

Hansen has found that a growing number of well-known and successful companies are recognizing the benefits that incorporating mindfulness principles into their workplace culture can have. Apple, Google, McKinsey & Company, Deutsche Bank, Procter & Gamble, Astra Zeneca, General Mills, and Aetna have all implemented mindfulness programs for their employees. Many are already noticing pretty astounding results.

According to the Forbes article, General Mills reports that after a seven-week mindfulness training seminar, "83 per cent of participants said they were 'taking time each day to optimize my personal productivity' — up from 23 per cent before the course. Eighty-two per cent said they now make time to eliminate tasks with limited productivity value — up from 32 per cent before the course. And among senior executives who took the course, 80 per cent reported a positive change in their ability to make better decisions, while 89 per cent said they became better listeners."

Hansen goes on to find that the leaders of Silicon Valley are firm supporters of mindfulness meditation and how it can help them to better lead their companies. They have identified meditation practices that they incorporate into their daily business lives:

1. "Anchor your day with a contemplative morning practice (e.g., Breath, Zen, Kabbala, etc.)
2. Before entering the workplace, remind yourself of your organization's purpose and recommit to your vocation as a leader
3. Throughout the day, pause to be fully present in the moment before undertaking the next critical task
4. Review the day's events at the close of the day to prevent work stresses from spilling into your home life
5. Before going to bed, engage in some spiritual reading"[xxviii]

Finally, Google has implemented a mindfulness program with its employees which it has now begun to share with others. According to Hansen: "Led by Chade-Meng Tan, its Jolly Good Fellow, Google introduced a program to increase emotional intelligence using mindfulness — and backed by scientific research. It's called Search Inside Yourself and is now offered to organizations outside the Googleplex.

Even successful businesses are now seeing the benefits that mindfulness training and meditation have to offer their employees. Increasing the emotional awareness of employees creates a more positive workplace environment and leads to greater productivity.

Now the question becomes how we incorporate mindfulness principles into our workplace on a daily basis. Here are a few easy suggestions that anyone can begin to implement immediately.

How many times have you dreaded going into a meeting thinking that you were going to hear something negative, or that it was just going to be a big waste of time? The first way we can improve our workplace environment is by shifting our way of thinking. Instead of expecting the worse, we can wish the meeting's leader the best. Send out a positive thought that they will have a productive and beneficial meeting. Not only will you have a more positive outlook, but now you are personally invested in the successful outcome of the meeting before it begins. This may lead you to be a better listener, or a more active and helpful participant in the meeting.

Another easy tip for implementing mindfulness in the workplace is simply to look people in the eye when you are speaking with them. This signals to your colleague that you value what they have to say and are focused solely on listening to them. It can also serve as a calming influence on both parties, should tensions arise during the conversation.

Taking a minute for meditation to take 10 deep breaths before you begin a new task can reset the connection and rhythm between your body and mind. This can help to make you focused and ready to take on any new task, feeling refreshed and productive.

Perhaps one of the simplest and most powerful ways we can improve our workplace environment for our colleagues and ourselves is just by smiling. You will find that your smile can instantly decrease everyone's stress levels and cause improved moods, making for a more enjoyable day at work for everyone involved.

Unfortunately, people naturally make judgments about the people and world around them. When you add in the often competitive nature of the workplace, these judgments can be even more magnified. Through our examination of mindfulness so far, we have learned that judging others and ourselves is a detriment that takes away our energy and focus from more important and productive matters. This is no exception in the workplace. We need to acknowledge and be aware that we are making these judgments and put them aside so that we can direct our attention where it should be.

Mindfulness is a powerful thing. We now know of even more benefits it has to enhance our lives, and perhaps more importantly, the little adjustments we can make to help ourselves take full advantage of all mindfulness has to offer.

## What is Mindfulness Based Stress Reduction?

Mindfulness Based Stress Reduction (MBSR) was developed in the 1970s at the University of Massachusetts Medical Center by Professor Jon Kabat-Zinn. In 1979, he went on to open the Mindfulness Stress Based Reduction Clinic at the University of Massachusetts Medical Center. MBSR uses yoga, body awareness, and mindfulness meditation in the hopes of helping people to become more mindful.

Kabat-Zinn described mindfulness as "moment-to-moment non-judgmental awareness." The goal of the MBSR program is to help people stop dwelling on the past and stop worrying too much about the future by teaching them how to focus on the present. It is believed that by giving their attention to the environment around them and how they react to it, they will be better equipped to cope with the challenges they face.

Mindfulness Based Stress Reduction seeks to help people with pain and other conditions which may at some point best be treated outside of the hospital setting. It strives to help people relax and reduce their stress to show improvements in their overall quality of life. Over the years MBSR has grown in popularity so much that it is now practiced in hospitals around the world. Nearly 80% of medical schools today offer some form of mindfulness training to their students. MBSR is now considered a form of complementary medicine and is often utilized in the field of oncology.[xxix]

## Does it Work?

Mindfulness Based Stress Reduction has been used to help treat people with a variety of health concerns such as chronic pain, eating disorders, mood disorder, anxiety disorder, ADHD, substance abuse disorder, depression in expectant mothers, and insomnia across all age groups and backgrounds. It can also be helpful to people who are having difficulty accepting and coping with the fact that they have a serious medical condition.

Scans of the brain have found that gray matter density changed in areas of the brain that involve regulating our emotions and learning and memory processing after practicing MBSR. Studies have also found an improvement in immune system functioning correlating to the practicing of MBSR. Practicing mindfulness meditation has proved helpful in reducing feelings of depression among expectant mothers and improving the bond they report feeling with their unborn children. This reduction in depression was also reported among people who suffered from chronic illness.

Researchers studied the response to pain in people who participated in MBSR compared to people who did not participate in the mindfulness meditation. Brain scans revealed that the brains of both groups indicated they noticed the pain equally, but the participants of MBSR didn't transfer it into a perceived pain signal, so they registered a feeling of pain 40-50% less often than the group who did not participate.

There are also more studies being conducted on the effectiveness of MBSR on other health concerns, but while the results are encouraging, they are too preliminary at this time to be conclusive.

There seems to be a small window of time when we can choose how we will react to the stress and pain we experience. If we are in the present, focused, and aware, we have a much better chance of choosing to respond in a more positive way. Thankfully, mindfulness gives us the ability to interrupt our autopilot habits and negative cycles that we would not have if we were unaware of what is happening in the present moment.[xxx]

## Some of the Most Popular MBSR Exercises and Techniques

There are many different ways to practice mindfulness. Here we will highlight a few of the most popular methods. The type of mindfulness you are trying to practice will help you to determine the technique that would best suit your needs.

The first type of mindfulness is Focus Mindfulness. Since focus is the emphasis of this type, the goal is to look inward and be attentive to what is going on in your mind. You are laser-focused on one experience. In order to maintain this intense focus, breathing is most often the method of choice for keeping yourself grounded.

that focuses on the external more than the internal. It also focuses on the mind, but more as if you are a neutral observer looking in on it from the outside without passing any judgment. To practice this type of mindfulness, you would begin by focusing on your breaths. Then you would attempt to look upon your thoughts, moods, and feelings as if they are separate from you and just passing by. You then choose one thought or emotion to focus on for a bit and quiet all of the others into the background. Finally, you let go of the one you focused on and just leave it behind.[xxxi]

One of the techniques we have previously discussed in this book is breathing. It helps people achieve mindfulness by focusing on their rate of inhalation and exhalation.

The body scan is a popular technique that involves you lying flat on your back. You start at your toes and move your awareness all through your body, focusing on one area at a time. If you come across an area that feels tight or sore, you focus your breath and concentration on that area until it relaxes and then you move onto the next area.

Object meditation is a technique where you choose an object that has special meaning to you or that attention of all of your senses onto the object and receive the information that your senses send to your brain about the object, including its size, shape, weight, texture, sound, taste, and smell.

Mindful eating is a technique very similar to object meditation, except your focus is now on a food as you eat it slowly and notice everything about it.

Walking Meditation is a technique that involves you taking a stroll at a relaxed, gentle, and familiar pace. You focus all of your attention on how the different parts of your body feel as you walk and the way that your body moves. You try to make your breathing match your steps.

Simply Watching is a technique that only includes you and your thoughts. You don't really focus on your thoughts in this exercise. Instead you just watch them as if they are balloons floating through the sky without making any judgments about them. It may help to "announce" (vocalize) each thought as you visualize passing by (ex: Mom, hungry, laundry, chocolate chip cookies, stiff neck, etc.).

Worry or Urge "Surfing" is a technique where you think of your thoughts as waves of water you are "surfing" on. You direct your awareness toward the might be popping into your mind. You imagine those negative thoughts as a wave that gets bigger and bigger until it reaches you. Then you visualize yourself successfully riding the wave and watching the negative feelings continue to move away with the wave once it passes you by. This allows you to let go of the negativity instead of dwelling on it.[xxxii]

We have highlighted a great many benefits to Mindfulness Based Stress Reduction in this chapter. I believe in the power of the guiding principles to impact people in a positive way. I do not want to encourage or deter anyone from participating in the eight-week mindfulness course, and I am not tied by any personal or monetary interest in recommending it. I sincerely believe that whether or not to take the course is a personal decision that should be made by each individual after assessing their own unique risks and responsibilities. If, after giving it some thought, you decide that you want to try participating in a mindfulness course, there are opportunities available to you.

You could begin by conducting a simple internet search for MBSR teachers near you who received their certification from the Center for Mindfulness. There are also some online courses offered. The that follows the same method as the Center for Mindfulness and the teachings of Jon Kabat-Zinn. Another online course is offered by Palouse Mindfulness from a MBSR-certified instructor who trained at the University of Massachusetts Medical School. This course is based on the teachings of Kabat-Zinn, but it is not an exact copy of his work. These are just a few of the course offerings that are available. Many more can be found.

Mindfulness Based Stress Reduction is a program that has had proven success in helping people with a variety of health concerns. There are many benefits that everyone can experience from it, even if you are not suffering from a serious illness or pain. The varying techniques that can be used to practice mindfulness make it something that anyone can have success with if they choose to put forth the effort.

Mindfulness is an ability that we all possess, which allows us to be fully present and aware of where we are and what we are doing without being overwhelmed by what is happening around us. It is a way of life in which we make a conscious effort to quiet distractions and negative thoughts that creep into our minds and prevent us from being at our best. Mindfulness allows us to live in the present instead of being consumed by regrets or depression from the past, or worry and anxiety over the future.

Practicing mindfulness offers so many benefits to us, from improving our brain function and immune system to strengthening our relationships and allowing us the opportunity to stop being so hard on ourselves, and to stop listening to the negative mental chatter which stands in the way of us reaching our full potential, and so much more.

our own way, stopping our constant worrying, and going with the natural flow to accomplish more by doing less. Mindfulness supports our ability to do all of these things.

We discovered that practicing mindfulness and goal setting are not mutually exclusive, and in fact, both contribute to our growth. We now know the importance of shedding our preconceived notions of the way things should be and accepting things for the way they are in the present moment.

Mindfulness is truly impactful in all areas of our lives. It is my sincere hope that you will have read something in this book that will encourage you to look within yourself and find your own motivation to begin your journey to practicing mindfulness. I wish you good luck and great awareness as you embark on a truly rewarding new way of life.


—Steven

Academia, Edu. Mindfulness. Meditation Improves Cognition. 2015. https://s3.amazonaws.com/academia.edu.documents/39616081/Mindfulness_meditation_improves_cognitio20151102-1793-1onmb2t.pdf?AWSAccessKeyId=AKIAIWOWYYGZ2Y53UL3A&Expires=1504683231&Signature=WpYNB6oJIb9foH3IbWAFxcFyVs8%3D&response-content-disposition=inline%3B%20filename%3DMindfulness_meditation_improves_cognitio.pdf

Ackerman, Courtney. MBSR: 25 Mindfulness-Based Stress Reduction Exercises and Courses. Positive Psychology Program. 2017. https://positivepsychologyprogram.com/mindfulness-based-stress-reduction-mbsr/

Albertson, Ellen R., Neff, Kristin D., Dill-Shackleford, Karen E. Self-Compassion and Body Dissatisfaction in Women: A Randomized Controlled Trial of a Brief

https://link.springer.com/article/10.1007/s12671-014-0277-3#page-1

American Psychological Association. Delaying Gratification. American Psychological Association. https://www.apa.org/helpcenter/willpower-gratification.pdf

Atkinson Pain Research Laboratory, Division of Neurosurgery, Barrow Neurological Institute. Interoception: the sense of the physiological condition of the body. Pub Med. 2003. https://www.ncbi.nlm.nih.gov/pubmed/12965300

Barnes, S., et al. (2007). The role of mindfulness in romantic relationship satisfaction and response to relationship stress. Journal of Marital and Family Therapy, 33(4), 482-500.

Baum, Wil. LCSW. Mindfulness-Based Stress Reduction: What it Is, How it Helps. Psychology Today. 2010. https://www.psychologytoday.com/blog/crisis-knocks/201003/mindfulness-based-stress-reduction-what-it-is-how-it-helps

Center for Anxiety and Traumatic Stress Disorders. Randomized controlled trial of mindfulness meditation for generalized anxiety disorder: effects on anxiety and stress reactivity. Pub Med. 2013. https://www.ncbi.nlm.nih.gov/pubmed/23541163

Colier, Nancy. LCSW. Why Our Thoughts Are Not Real. Psychology Today. 2013. https://www.psychologytoday.com/blog/inviting-monkey-tea/201308/why-our-thoughts-are-not-real

Davidson, R., et al. (2003). Alterations in Brain and Immune Function Produced by Mindfulness Meditation. Psychosomatic Medicine, 65, 564-570.

Flook, L., Smalley, S.L., Kitil, M.J., Dang, J., Cho, J., Kaiser-Greenland, S., Locke, J. & Kasari, C. (2008, April). A mindful awareness practice improves executive function in preschool children.

Greenberg, Melanie. PhD. Five Ways Living Mindfully Can Help You Reach Your Goals. Psychology Today. 2013. https://www.psychologytoday.com/blog/the-

Greenberg, Melanie. PhD. Can Mindfulness Make Your Relationship Happier? Psychology Today. 2016. https://www.psychologytoday.com/blog/the-mindful-self-express/201606/can-mindfulness-make-your-relationship-happier

Hansen, Drew. A Guide To Mindfulness At Work. Forbes. 2012. https://www.forbes.com/sites/drewhansen/2012/10/31/a-guide-to-mindfulness-at-work/#6d94217825d2

Johnson. 44 Self Discipline Strategies, Backed By Science. 1 Percent Braver. 2016. http://1percentbraver.com/self-discipline/

Katherine A. MacLean, Emilio Ferrer, Stephen R. Aichele, David A. Bridwell, Anthony P. Zanesco, Tonya L. Jacobs, Brandon G. King, Erika L. Rosenberg, Baljinder K. Sahdra, Phillip R. Shaver, B. Alan Wallace, George R. Mangun, Clifford D. Saron. Intensive Meditation Training Improves Perceptual Discrimination and Sustained Attention. Sage

http://journal.sagepub.com/doi/abs/10.1177/0956
797610371339

Lazar, S., et al. (2005). Meditation experience is associated with increased cortical thickness. NeuroReport, 16(17), 1893-1897.

Lueke, Adam. Gibson, Brian. Mindfulness Meditation Reduces Implicit Age and Race Bias The Role of Reduced Automaticity of Responding. Sage Journals. 2014. http://journals.sagepub.com/doi/abs/10.1177/1948 550614559651

Manson, Mark. WHY I'M WRONG ABOUT EVERYTHING (AND SO ARE YOU). Mark Manson. 2013. https://markmanson.net/wrong-about-everything

McGonigall, Kelly. PhD. The Problem with Progress: Why Succeeding at Your Goals Can Sabotage Your Willpower. Psychology Today. 2011. https://www.psychologytoday.com/blog/the-science-willpower/201112/the-problem-progress-why-succeeding-your-goals-can-sabotage-your

McCreavey, Sue. Turn down the volume. Harvard Gazette. 2011. http://news.harvard.edu/gazette/story/2011/04/turn-down-the-volume/

Napoli, M., Krech, P., & Holley, L. (2005). Mindfulness Training for Elementary School Students: The Attention Academy. Journal of Applied School Psychology, 21(1), 99-125.

Pickert K (February 2014). "The art of being mindful. Finding peace in a stressed-out, digitally dependent culture may just be a matter of thinking differently". Time. 183 (4): 40–6.

Ravenscraft, Eric. Make Friends With Your Future Self to Get Better at Future Planning. Lifehacker. 2015. http://lifehacker.com/make-friends-with-your-future-self-to-get-better-at-fut-1750265016

Richards, Chip. Wu Wei: The Ancient Art of Non-Doing. Uplift. 2016. http://upliftconnect.com/wu-wei-ancient-art-non-doing/

Aggression, Noncompliance, and Self injury in
Children with Autism. Journal of Emotional and
Behavioral Disorders, 14(3), 169-177.


Staff, Mindful. What is Mindfulness? Mindful. 2014.
https://www.mindful.org/what-is-mindfulness/


Teo, Soon. DO NOTHING if you want to be your
best. Tao in you. 2016. http://tao-in-you.com/do-
nothing-is-doing-something/

[i] Staff, Mindful. What is Mindfulness? Mindful. 2014. https://www.mindful.org/what-is-mindfulness/

[ii] Lazar, S., et al. (2005). Meditation experience is associated with increased cortical thickness. NeuroReport, 16(17), 1893-1897.

[iii] Davidson, R., et al. (2003). Alterations in Brain and Immune Function Produced by Mindfulness Meditation. Psychosomatic Medicine, 65, 564-570.

[iv] Tang, Y., et al. (2007). Short-term meditation training improves attention and self-regulation. PNAS, 104(43), 17152-17156.

[v] Barnes, S., et al. (2007). The role of mindfulness in romantic relationship satisfaction and response to relationship

Therapy, 33(4), 482-500.

[vi] Singh, N., et al. (2006). Mindful Parenting Decreases Aggression, Noncompliance, and Self-Injury in Children with Autism. Journal of Emotional and Behavioral Disorders, 14(3), 169-177.

[vii] Napoli, M., Krech, P., & Holley, L. (2005). Mindfulness Training for Elementary School Students: The Attention Academy. Journal of Applied School Psychology, 21(1), 99-125.

[viii] Flook, L., Smalley, S.L., Kitil, M.J., Dang, J., Cho, J., Kaiser-Greenland, S., Locke, J. & Kasari, C. (2008, April). A mindful awareness practice improves executive function in preschool children.

[ix] Center for Anxiety and Traumatic Stress Disorders. Randomized controlled trial of mindfulness meditation for generalized anxiety disorder: effects on anxiety and stress reactivity. Pub Med. 2013. https://www.ncbi.nlm.nih.gov/pubmed/235 41163

[x] Lueke, Adam. Gibson, Brian. Mindfulness Meditation Reduces Implicit Age and Race Bias
The Role of Reduced Automaticity of Responding. Sage Journals. 2014. http://journals.sagepub.com/doi/abs/10.11 77/1948550614559651

Shackleford, Karen E. Self-Compassion and Body Dissatisfaction in Women: A Randomized Controlled Trial of a Brief Meditation Intervention. Springer link. Original paper: Mindfulness, Volume 6, Issue 3, pp. 444–454. 2015. https://link.springer.com/article/10.1007/s12671-014-0277-3#page-1

[xii] Academia, Edu. Mindfulness. Meditation Improves Cognition. 2015. https://s3.amazonaws.com/academia.edu.documents/39616081/Mindfulness_meditation_improves_cognitio20151102-1793-1onmb2t.pdf?AWSAccessKeyId=AKIAIWOWYYGZ2Y53UL3A&Expires=1504683231&Signature=WpYNB6oJIb9foH3IbWAFxcFyVs8%3D&response-content-disposition=inline%3B%20filename%3DMindfulness_meditation_improves_cognitio.pdf

[xiii] Haliwell, Ed. Meditate With Intention, Not Goals. Mindful. 2015. https://www.mindful.org/meditate-with-intention-not-goals/

[xiv] Katherine A. MacLean, Emilio Ferrer, Stephen R. Aichele, David A. Bridwell, Anthony P. Zanesco, Tonya L. Jacobs, Brandon G. King, Erika L. Rosenberg, Baljinder K. Sahdra, Phillip R. Shaver, B. Alan Wallace, George R. Mangun, Clifford D.

Improves Perceptual Discrimination and Sustained Attention. Sage Journals. 2010. http://journals.sagepub.com/doi/abs/10.1177/0956797610371339

[xv] American Psychological Association. Delaying Gratification. American Psychological Association. https://www.apa.org/helpcenter/willpower-gratification.pdf

[xvi] Ravenscraft, Eric. Make Friends With Your Future Self to Get Better at Future Planning. Lifehacker. 2015. http://lifehacker.com/make-friends-with-your-future-self-to-get-better-at-fut-1750265016

[xvii] McGonigall, Kelly. PhD. The Problem with Progress: Why Succeeding at Your Goals Can Sabotage Your Willpower. Psychology Today. 2011. https://www.psychologytoday.com/blog/the-science-willpower/201112/the-problem-progress-why-succeeding-your-goals-can-sabotage-your

[xviii] Johnson. 44 Self Discipline Strategies, Backed By Science. 1 Percent Braver. 2016. http://1percentbraver.com/self-discipline/

[xix] McGreevey, Sue. 'Turn down the volume.' Harvard Gazette. 2011.

4/turn-down-the-volume/

[xx] Colier, Nancy. LCSW. Why Our Thoughts Are Not Real. Psychology Today. 2013. https://www.psychologytoday.com/blog/inviting-monkey-tea/201308/why-our-thoughts-are-not-real

[xxi] Manson, Mark. WHY I'M WRONG ABOUT EVERYTHING (AND SO ARE YOU). Mark Manson. 2013. https://markmanson.net/wrong-about-everything

[xxii] Atkinson Pain Research Laboratory, Division of Neurosurgery, Barrow Neurological Institute. Interoception: the sense of the physiological condition of the body. Pub Med. 2003. https://www.ncbi.nlm.nih.gov/pubmed/12965300

[xxiii] Teo, Soon. DO NOTHING if you want to be your best. Tao in you. 2016. http://tao-in-you.com/do-nothing-is-doing-something/

[xxiv] Richards, Chip. Wu Wei: The Ancient Art of Non-Doing. Uplift. 2016. http://upliftconnect.com/wu-wei-ancient-art-non-doing/

[xxv] Greenberg, Melanie. PhD. Five Ways Living Mindfully Can Help You Reach Your Goals. Psychology Today. 2013. https://www.psychologytoday.com/blog/th

living-mindfully-can-help-you-reach-your-goals

[xxvi] Greenberg, Melanie. PhD. Can Mindfulness Make Your Relationship Happier? Psychology Today. 2016. https://www.psychologytoday.com/blog/the-mindful-self-express/201606/can-mindfulness-make-your-relationship-happier

[xxvii] Hansen, Drew. A Guide To Mindfulness At Work. Forbes. 2012. https://www.forbes.com/sites/drewhansen/2012/10/31/a-guide-to-mindfulness-at-work/#6d94217825d2

[xxviii] Hansen, Drew. A Guide To Mindfulness At Work. Forbes. 2012. https://www.forbes.com/sites/drewhansen/2012/10/31/a-guide-to-mindfulness-at-work/#6d94217825d2

[xxix] Pickert K (February 2014). "The art of being mindful. Finding peace in a stressed-out, digitally dependent culture may just be a matter of thinking differently". Time. 183 (4): 40–6.

[xxx] Baum, Wil. LCSW. Mindfulness-Based Stress Reduction: What it Is, How it Helps. Psychology Today. 2010. https://www.psychologytoday.com/blog/cri

stress-reduction-what-it-is-how-it-helps

[xxxi] Ackerman, Courtney. MBSR: 25 Mindfulness-Based Stress Reduction Exercises and Courses. Positive Psychology Program. 2017. https://positivepsychologyprogram.com/mindfulness-based-stress-reduction-mbsr/

[xxxii] Ackerman, Courtney. MBSR: 25 Mindfulness-Based Stress Reduction Exercises and Courses. Positive Psychology Program. 2017. https://positivepsychologyprogram.com/mindfulness-based-stress-reduction-mbsr/

Made in the USA
Monee, IL
18 November 2019